PARSLEY

PARSLEY

A BOOK OF RECIPES

EDITED BY: HELEN SUDELL

LORENZ BOOKS

First published in 2014 by Lorenz Books
an imprint of Anness Publishing Limited
108 Great Russell Street, London WC1B 3NA
www.annesspublishing.com
www.lorenzbooks.com; info@anness.com

If you like the images in this book and would like to investigate
using them for publishing, promotions or advertising, please visit
our website www.practicalpictures.com for more information

A CIP catalogue record for this book is available from
The British Library

Publisher Joanna Lorenz
Editorial Director Helen Sudell
Designer Nigel Partridge
Illustrations Anna Koska

Printed and bound in China

COOK'S NOTES

• Bracketed terms are intended for American readers.

• For all recipes, quantities are given in both metric and imperial
measures and, where appropriate, in standard cups and spoons.
Follow one set of measures, but not a mixture, because they are
not interchangeable.

• Standard spoon and cup measures are level. 1 tsp = 5ml,
1 tbsp = 15ml, 1 cup = 250ml/8fl oz.

• Australian standard tablespoons are 20ml. Australian readers
should use 3 tsp in place of 1 tbsp for measuring small quantities.

• American pints are 16fl oz/2 cups. American readers should use
20fl oz/2.5 cups in place of 1 pint when measuring liquids.

• Electric oven temperatures in this book are for conventional
ovens. When using a fan oven, the temperature will probably need
to be reduced by about 10–20°C/20–40°F. Since ovens vary, you
should check with your manufacturer's instruction book for
guidance.

• The nutritional analysis given for each recipe is calculated per
portion (i.e. serving or item), unless otherwise stated. If the recipe
gives a range, such as Serves 4–6, then the nutritional analysis will
be for the smaller portion size, i.e. 6 servings. The analysis does not
include optional ingredients, such as salt added to taste.

• Medium (US large) eggs are used unless otherwise stated.

PUBLISHER'S NOTE

Although the advice and information in this book are believed to
be accurate and true at the time of going to press, neither the
authors nor the publisher can accept any legal responsibility or
liability for any errors or omissions that may have been made nor
for any inaccuracies nor for any loss, harm or injury that comes
about from following instructions or advice in this book.

CONTENTS

INTRODUCTION

Parsley has a very special place in the kitchen. Its mild, unassuming flavour makes it the most versatile of herbs, adding a fine delicacy to an almost limitless number of savoury dishes. Many herbs make their presence known in quite forceful ways, and cuisines such as Italian, Turkish and Thai can be defined by their well-flavoured aromatic or pungent herbs. Yet in all these cuisines,

Below: Parsley makes a fine sauce to serve with fish .

parsley is never forgotten. It may play a quieter, more modest role than its racier cousins, but it is still among the most widely used of herbs, appreciated for its subtle aromatic flavour and its vibrant green colour.

Native to southern Europe, parsley was grown by the ancient Greeks, who used the herb for ceremonial and medicinal purposes as well as in salads and sauces. The Romans appreciated parsley as a food and brought it over to Britain where it flourished in the moderate climate.

Enthusiasm for parsley continued throughout the centuries. Since it could be grown so successfully in England it remained popular, unlike many of the herbs introduced from southern Europe. During the Middle Ages, people would have grown the herb both for culinary and medicinal uses, as it was

Above: Parsley is often added at the end of cooking as a garnish.

considered useful for a number of ailments. This reputation has found its way into stories too. Beatrix Potter's Peter Rabbit, after gorging himself in Mr McGregor's vegetable garden, nibbles on parsley to settle his stomach! Indeed, parsley is one of the most nutritious of herbs. It is particularly high in carotene and vitamin C and contains useful amounts of potassium and calcium. If chewed it can mask the smell of garlic on the breath.

There are three main varieties of parsley. Curly parsley grows most successfully in northern climates and is the most popular. Flat-leaf or Italian parsley is a less hardy plant and grows best in the warmer climates of southern Europe and the Middle East, where it is used in huge quantities. Turnip-rooted or Hamburg parsley, although a member of the same family, is not used as a herb, but its roots are eaten as a vegetable.

Below: Flat-leaf parsley has attractive, lacy leaves.

GROWING PARSLEY

Parsley will grow happily in a warm place outside the kitchen door, or on the windowsill. It needs plenty of sun, and on warm days should be kept watered. To grow your own parsley, soak the seeds overnight and then sow directly into pots or into the earth in early spring. The soil must be watered regularly with a fine spray during germination. Once the seedlings are big enough to handle, they should be thinned until the plants are about 20cm/8in apart. Parsley seeds are notoriously slow to germinate so be patient. Parsley can be kept indoors on a kitchen windowsill or outside, in pots and hanging baskets.

DRYING PARSLEY

Although fresh parsley is vastly superior, it is useful to dry any excess you have in summer to use in the winter. Tie bundles of fresh parsley and hang from a rack in a warm, dry room. Leave for a week, until the leaves are

Above: Grow parsley in a large pot with other kitchen herbs.

crisp and dry. To keep the parsley dust-free, place brown paper bags over the tops of the bunches, leaving the bottom open to allow air to circulate. Once completely dry, strip the leaves from the stem and place in a jar. Close and check the next day for condensation, which indicates that the leaves are not completely dry. If this is so place the parsley on a rack lined with muslin (cheesecloth) and leave in a warm room for 24 hours. Store in airtight dark jars.

TYPES OF PARSLEY

CURLY PARSLEY

Often called English parsley, this is the most common parsley and is certainly the most easily recognized. It has dark emerald green leaves that vary between very curled and softly curled. It has a good, fresh flavour and is particularly popular as a garnish.

FLAT-LEAF PARSLEY

Also known as Italian parsley, this is the most favoured parsley in European countries, particularly France, Spain and Italy. It has pretty, rather lacy, leaves, varying in colour from pale to dark green. It has a more pronounced flavour that is pleasantly aromatic, giving salads and cooked dishes a distinct yet fresh taste. It also makes an attractive garnish.

TURNIP-ROOTED PARSLEY

This plant is grown mainly for its tapering root which looks rather like a thin parsnip and tastes like a cross betweem celeriac and parsley. It is also sometimes referred to as Hamburg parsley and, as the name suggests, the plant is popular in Germany where it is used as a root vegetable.

DRIED PARSLEY

You can buy dried parsley from a local supermarket, or you can dry your own very easily. Commercially dried parsley has a reputation for having little or

Below: Freshly chopped herbs are one of the joys of cooking.

no flavour, although it is obviously acceptable if there is no alternative and if it is used shortly after opening. Store dried parsley in a cool dry place. Once opened, use within 2–3 months – after this time the flavour will start to deteriorate quite quickly.

FROZEN PARSLEY

Flat-leaf and curly parsley are available frozen, or you can freeze your own. Commercially frozen parsley comes in conveniently small containers or zip bags that can be re-sealed. Do not allow the frozen parsley to defrost and then re-freeze, as this could introduce potentially harmful bacteria as well as destroying flavour.

CHOPPED PARSLEY

Parsley is chopped both in cooking and for garnishing. It can be finely or coarsely chopped, either with a sharp knife or using a herb mill.

Dried parsley

Flat-leaf parsley

Curly parsley

Frozen chopped parsley

Fresh chopped parsley

COOKING WITH PARSLEY

Parsley is a versatile herb and can be chopped and added to a dish, made into a sauce, tied with other fresh herbs as part of a bouquet garni, or used as a garnish.

HARVESTING PARSLEY

As with any fresh herb, parsley is best harvested first thing in the morning before the hot sun has dried out the leaves. Ideally try to cut only what you need to use at one time. If you are not ready to use all of your picked parsley immediately, submerge the cut ends in cold water and store in a cool place. Alternatively, you can wrap the leaves loosely in a plastic bag and chill in the refrigerator.

Always wash your parsley thoroughly before use, shaking the excess water off the leaves. To dry the parsley completely place the leaves on a paper towel, cover with another one, then press together gently. Repeat if necessary.

STRIPPING PARSLEY FROM ITS STEM

To strip the leaves from the stems before cooking, hold the sprig at the tip and strip off the leaves with your fingers. Discard the stems.

CHOPPING PARSLEY

To chop by hand, snip the leaves from the stalks and chop coarsely, bunching the leaves up against a knife. You can also

use a herb mill or a coffee mill for small quantities of parsley, and a food processor for larger quantities.

MAKING A BOUQUET GARNI

A bouquet garni is useful when you want the flavour of the herbs but do not want them to show in the finished dish.

A classic bouquet garni comprises parsley stalks, a sprig of thyme and a bay leaf tied together with string. Another method is to wrap the herbs in squares of muslin (cheesecloth). Break or tear the herbs into small pieces and place in the centre of a 10–13cm/4–5in square of clean muslin. Bring

the edges of the muslin up over the herbs and tie the ends firmly with a length of string. Use the excess string to tie the bundle to the pan handle for ease of removal.

FREEZING PARSLEY

Wash fresh parsley sprigs and shake dry carefully. Place in freezer bags, label and freeze. For chopped parsley, place a tablespoon in ice cube trays and top up with water. The frozen cubes can be added directly to cooked dishes.

PARSLEY SAUCE

Parsley sauce is a classic recipe that is used in all sorts of meat, fish and vegetarian dishes.

1 Melt 40g/1½ oz/3 tbsp butter in a saucepan. Add 20g/¾ oz/2 tbsp plain (all-purpose) flour and cook gently for one minute, stirring often.

2 Gradually stir in 425ml/ ¾ pint/1¾ cups milk, beating until smooth after each addition, to make a smooth shiny sauce. Cook very gently for about 1 minute.

3. Stir in 45ml/3 tbsp finely chopped fresh parsley and season to taste. For a richer parsley sauce, add 15ml/1 tbsp single (light) cream.

PARSLEY COOKING TIPS

• The more densely curled the parsley, the better it is for cooking. Flat-leaf parsley is always chopped before being added to dishes.
• In sauces, add parsley at the last minute so that it simply heats through. As a general rule, parsley should only be heated, not cooked.
• An exception to the above is to deep-fry sprigs of parsley and serve them as a fantastic starter or garnish.

Stir in 60ml/4 tbsp finely chopped fresh parsley into the sauce, then spoon into sterilized jars. Seal and store in the refrigerator. It will keep for 2–3 weeks, but once opened, it should be used within 3 days.

CHIMICHURRI

This Argentinian classic is used as both a marinade and a sauce. It is a must for serving with grilled steak.

Makes 300ml/½ pint/1¼ cups
Mix together 1 finely chopped onion, 5 finely chopped garlic cloves, 2.5ml/½ tsp dried chilli flakes, 5ml/1 tsp dried oregano, 5ml/1 tsp paprika, 5ml/1 tsp salt and 2.5ml/½ tsp ground black pepper. Add 15ml/1 tbsp lemon juice and 75ml/2½ fl oz/⅓ cup red wine vinegar, then stir in 150ml/¼ pint/⅔ cup extra virgin olive oil a little at a time.

PERSILLADE

For a fresh Provençal flavour add this classic French seasoning to fish and poultry dishes just before serving.

Makes 60ml/4 tbsp
Very finely chop 60ml/4 tbsp fresh flat-leaf parsley and mix with 2 very finely chopped cloves of garlic. Add a good pinch of sea salt and mix well.

GREMOLATA

This Italian flavouring is made from very fine lemon rind, garlic and parsley. It is traditionally sprinkled over Osso Buco (an Italian dish of braised veal shanks with vegetables), but can be used as a garnish for any rich, braised meat dishes.

Makes 60ml/4 tbsp
Mix together 60ml/4 tbsp finely chopped fresh parsley and 2 finely chopped garlic cloves. Using a lemon zester add fine strands of lemon rind and mix together well. Cover and keep in the refrigerator until ready to use.

PARSLEY AND CAPER SAUCE

This popular Mediterranean sauce is great with fish.

Makes 75ml/5 tbsp/⅓ cup
Place 45ml/3 tbsp fresh flat-leaf parsley, 1 garlic clove and 2 shallots in a food processor. Soak a slice of day-old bread in water, squeeze dry and add to the bowl with 10ml/1 tsp rinsed capers and 30ml/2 tbsp white wine vinegar. Add 75ml/ 5 tbsp olive oil, season and process until well combined but not completely smooth. Pour into a bowl, cover and leave to infuse for 1 hour before serving.

PARSLEY BUTTER

Add freshly chopped parsley to creamy butter to serve with grilled (broiled) fish to add extra flavour.

Makes 115g/4 oz
Mash 115g/4 oz softened unsalted butter and blend with ½ crushed garlic clove, 15ml/ 1 tbsp lemon juice and 45ml/ 3 tbsp chopped fresh parsley. Shape into a log and roll up in baking parchment. Chill and slice as required.

PARSLEY STUFFING

Create a tasty herb stuffing to serve with roast lamb, turkey, chicken or game birds.

Makes 150g/5 oz/⅔ cup
Fry 3 snipped slices of streaky (fatty) bacon with 1 finely chopped onion in a little butter. Mix with 115g/4 oz fresh breadcrumbs and 1 diced apple. Add 45ml/3 tbsp chopped fresh parsley and season well. Moisten with lemon juice and a little chicken stock if necessary.

PARSLEY AND THYME OIL

This herby oil is perfect for green salads and stir-fries.

Makes 600ml/1 pint/2½ cups
Pour 600ml/1 pint/2½ cups extra virgin olive oil into a sterilized jar and add 50g/ 2oz/½ cup each of chopped fresh parsley and thyme. Cover and allow to stand for 1 week. Shake occasionally. Strain the oil through a fine sieve lined with muslin (cheesecloth) into a sterilized container and then decant into sterilized bottles, discarding the used herbs. Store in a cool place and use within 6 months.

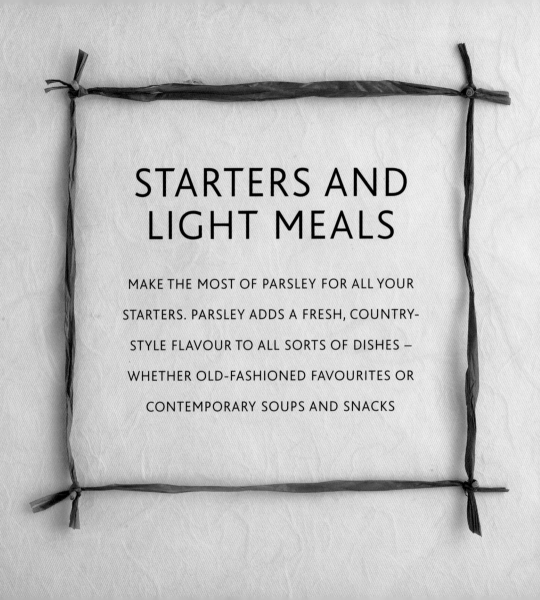

STARTERS AND LIGHT MEALS

MAKE THE MOST OF PARSLEY FOR ALL YOUR STARTERS. PARSLEY ADDS A FRESH, COUNTRY-STYLE FLAVOUR TO ALL SORTS OF DISHES – WHETHER OLD-FASHIONED FAVOURITES OR CONTEMPORARY SOUPS AND SNACKS

CHICKPEA AND PARSLEY SOUP

A hearty winter soup that is easy to make. Chickpeas blend better in soups and other dishes if the outer skin is rubbed away with your fingers, so it is well worth doing.

Serves 6

225g/8oz/1⅓ cups chickpeas, soaked overnight
1 small onion
1 bunch fresh parsley (about 40g/1½ oz)
30ml/2 tbsp olive and sunflower oil, mixed
1.2 litres/2 pints/5 cups chicken stock
juice of ½ lemon
salt and ground black pepper
lemon wedges and finely pared strips of rind, to garnish

Drain the chickpeas and rinse under cold water. Cook them in boiling water for 1–1½ hours until tender. Drain and peel.

Place the onion and parsley in a food processor or blender and process until finely chopped.

Heat the olive and sunflower oils in a saucepan and fry the onion mixture for about 4 minutes until the onion is slightly softened.

Add the chickpeas, cook gently for 1–2 minutes and add the stock. Season well. Bring the soup to the boil, then cover and simmer for 20 minutes until the chickpeas are very tender.

Allow the soup to cool a little and then part-purée in a food processor or blender, so that the soup is thick but still quite chunky.

Return the soup to a clean pan and add the lemon juice. Heat gently and then serve garnished with lemon wedges and finely pared rind.

Energy 140kcal/591kJ; Protein 8.1g; Carbohydrate 19.4g, of which sugars 1.5g; Fat 2.9g, of which saturates 0.5g; Cholesterol 0mg; Calcium 63mg; Fibre 4.2g; Sodium 15mg.

SPICED RED LENTIL SOUP WITH PARSLEY CREAM

Crispy shallots and a parsley cream top this rich soup, which is inspired by an Indian dhal. Chunks of smoked bacon add texture and extra flavour.

Serves 6

5ml/1 tsp cumin seeds
2.5ml/½ tsp coriander seeds
5ml/1 tsp ground turmeric
30ml/2 tbsp olive oil
1 onion, chopped
2 garlic cloves, chopped
1 smoked bacon hock
1.2 litres/2 pints/5 cups
    vegetable stock
275g/10oz/1¼ cups red lentils
400g/14oz can chopped
    tomatoes
15ml/1 tbsp vegetable oil
3 shallots, thinly sliced

For the parsley cream

45ml/3 tbsp fresh parsley,
    chopped
150ml/¼ pint/⅔ cup Greek
    (US-strained plain) yogurt
salt and ground black pepper

Energy 235kcal/991kJ; Protein 13g;
Carbohydrate 28.4g, of which sugars 3.7g;
Fat 8.9g, of which saturates 2.2g;
Cholesterol 130mg; Calcium 66mg; Fibre
2.9g; Sodium 40mg.

Heat a frying pan and add the cumin and coriander seeds. Roast them over a high heat for a few seconds, shaking the pan until they smell aromatic. Transfer to a mortar and crush using a pestle. Mix in the turmeric and set aside.

Heat the oil in a large saucepan. Add the onion and garlic and cook for 4–5 minutes, until softened. Add the spice mixture and cook for 2 minutes, stirring continuously.

Place the bacon in the pan and pour in the stock. Bring to the boil, cover and simmer gently for 30 minutes.

Add the red lentils and cook for 20 minutes or until the lentils and bacon hock are tender. Stir in the tomatoes and cook for a further 5 minutes.

Remove the bacon from the pan and set it aside until cool enough to handle. Leave the soup to cool slightly, then process in a food processor or blender until almost smooth. You may have to do this in batches. Return the soup to the rinsed-out pan. Cut the meat from the hock, discarding skin and fat, then stir it into the soup and reheat.

Heat the vegetable oil in a frying pan and fry the shallots for 10 minutes until crisp and golden. Remove from the pan using a draining spoon and drain on kitchen paper.

To make the parsley cream, stir the chopped parsley into the yogurt and season well. Ladle the soup into bowls and add a dollop of the parsley cream to each. Pile some crisp shallots on to each portion and serve at once.

VEGETABLE SALAD WITH PARSLEY

Known as taze ezmesi *in Turkey, this refreshing salad is served as part of a traditional meze. It makes a tasty snack, and is good served with chunks of warm, crusty bread.*

Serves 4

2 large tomatoes, skinned, seeded and finely chopped
1 green (bell) pepper, seeded and finely chopped
1 onion, finely chopped
1 green chilli, seeded and finely chopped
1 small bunch fresh flat-leaf parsley, finely chopped
a few fresh mint leaves, finely chopped
15–30ml/1–2 tbsp olive oil
salt and ground black pepper

Energy 101kcal/420kJ; Protein 2.3g;
Carbohydrate 9.3g, of which sugars 8g;
Fat 6.3g, of which saturates 0.9g;
Cholesterol 0mg; Calcium 66mg; Fibre
2.7g; Sodium 15mg.

Put all the finely chopped ingredients in a bowl and mix well together.

Bind the mixture with oil and season with salt and pepper. Serve at room temperature, in individual bowls or one large dish.

TURNING THE SALAD INTO A PASTE

When you bind the vegetables with the olive oil, add 15–30ml/1–2 tbsp tomato purée (paste) with a little extra chilli and 5–10ml/1–2 tsp sugar. The mixture will become a tangy paste to spread on toasted pitta, and it can also be used as a sauce for grilled (broiled) or barbecued meats.

PARSLEY CORN ON THE COB

Keeping the husks on the corn protects the kernels and encloses the butter, so the flavours are contained. Fresh corn with husks intact are perfect, but a double layer of foil can also be used.

Serves 6

250g/9oz/generous 1 cup butter, softened
3 chipotle chillies, very finely chopped
7.5ml/1½ tsp lemon juice
45ml/3 tbsp fresh flat-leaf parsley, chopped
6 corn on the cob, with husks intact
salt and ground black pepper

Energy 164kcal/689kJ; Protein 4.2g;
Carbohydrate 20.1g, of which sugars 4g;
Fat 8g, of which saturates 1.1g; Cholesterol
248mg; Calcium 19mg; Fibre 2g; Sodium
44mg.

Place the butter in a bowl and add the chillies, lemon juice and parsley. Season to taste and mix well.

Peel back the husks from each cob without tearing them. Remove the silk. Smear about 30ml/2 tbsp of the chilli butter over each cob. Pull the husks back over the cobs, ensuring that the butter is well hidden. Put the rest of the butter in a pot, smooth the top and chill to use later. Place the cobs in a bowl of cold water and leave for 1–3 hours.

Prepare the barbecue. Remove the corn cobs from the water and wrap in pairs in foil. Once the flames have died down, position a lightly oiled grill rack over the coals to heat. When the coals have a moderate coating of ash, grill the corn for 15–20 minutes. Remove the foil and cook them for about 5 minutes more, turning them often to char the husks a little. Serve hot, with the rest of the butter.

SMOKED MACKEREL AND PARSLEY PÂTÉ

This recipe provides an ideal way to use smoked mackerel – it's quick and easy, involves no cooking and is extremely versatile. The parsley helps cut through the oily flavour of the mackerel.

Serves 4–6

225g/8oz/1 cup crème fraîche or Greek (US-strained plain) yogurt
finely grated rind of ½ lemon
few sprigs of parsley, plus extra chopped parsley to garnish
225g/8oz smoked mackerel fillets
5–10ml/1–2 tsp horseradish sauce
1 tbsp lemon juice, or to taste
ground black pepper
crusty bread, hot toast or crisp plain crackers, to serve
lemon wedges, to serve

Put the crème fraîche and lemon rind into a blender or food processor. Add a few sprigs of parsley.

Flake the mackerel, discarding the skin and any bones. Add the flaked fish to the blender. Blend on a medium speed until almost smooth.

Add the horseradish sauce and lemon juice and blend briefly. Season with pepper. Spoon into individual dishes. Cover and refrigerate until required.

Garnish with parsley and serve with crusty bread, hot toast or crackers and lemon wedges for squeezing over.

Energy 344kcal/1421kJ; Protein 10.7g; Carbohydrate 0.5g, of which sugars 0.4g; Fat 33.3g, of which saturates 14.3g; Cholesterol 88mg; Calcium 57mg; Fibre 0.1g; Sodium 518mg

FIERY CHEESE AND PARSLEY DIP

This meze dish is spiked with chilli powder and used to whet the appetite for the dishes to follow. It is traditionally very spicy so use less chilli powder if you prefer. Serve with warm flat bread.

Serves 3–4
250g/9oz feta cheese
15–30ml/1–2 tbsp Greek (US-strained plain) yogurt
5–10ml/1–2 tsp chilli powder
1 small bunch flat-leaf parsley, leaves finely chopped, plus 1 small bunch flat-leaf parsley, trimmed, to serve
salt
1 lemon, cut into wedges, to serve

In a bowl, mash the cheese with a fork, or process it in a food processor or blender. Beat in the yogurt, again using the fork or the blender, until the mixture is fairly smooth and creamy.

Add the chilli powder and the parsley. Taste the dip to see if you need to add any salt – often the cheese is sufficiently salty.

Spoon the cheese dip into a dish and serve as part of a *meze* spread with warm flat bread, such as pitta pouches, wedges of lemon to squeeze over each mouthful, and leafy stalks of flat leaf parsley to chew on, to cut the spice.

Energy 170kcal/705kJ; Protein 10.7g; Carbohydrate 2.4g, of which sugars 1.5g; Fat 13.2g, of which saturates 8.6g; Cholesterol 44mg; Calcium 262mg; Fibre 0.6g; Sodium 908mg.

VARIATIONS
• Crushed walnuts can be mixed into the dip in step 2, or sprinkled over the top, to add texture to the dip.
• Finely chopped fresh mint can be added to the parsley to give a refreshing lift to the dish.

FRITTATA WITH FRESH HERBS

A frittata made with plenty of fresh herbs is a delight at any time of year, but especially when the first spring shoots are plentiful. Serve the frittata either hot or cold with salad.

Serves 4

about 45ml/3 tbsp extra virgin olive oil
1 garlic bulb, cloves chopped
5 small spring onions (scallions), chopped
1 small bunch fresh mint leaves, chopped
1 small handful fresh lemon balm leaves, chopped
1 small handful fresh flat-leaf parsley leaves, chopped
1 small handful fresh chervil leaves, chopped
8 eggs
salt and ground black pepper
salad leaves, to serve

Put the oil in a non-stick frying pan and add 45ml/3 tbsp cold water. Add the garlic, spring onions, mint, lemon balm, flat-leaf parsley and chervil, and cook for 5 minutes, or until softened.

Beat the eggs together in a small bowl, then season them with salt and pepper.

Pour the beaten eggs into the frying pan with the herb mixture and stir gently with a wooden spoon to combine.

As the egg begins to set, rock the pan slightly from side to side and pull the outer edge of the frittata towards the centre, making sure the underneath of the frittata sets completely, without burning.

Cover the frittata with a plate that is larger than the pan. Turn it over in one smooth movement, so that it lands safely on the plate.

If the pan looks completely dry, add a little more oil, then slide the frittata back into the hot pan, starting at the opposite side of the pan and drawing the plate back towards you.

Shake the frittata into position, flatten gently with a spatula, and cook until golden brown underneath.

Slide the frittata out on to a platter and serve hot or cold, cut into wedges, with a green salad.

Energy 235kcal/975kJ; Protein 13.7g; Carbohydrate 1.7g, of which sugars 0.4g; Fat 19.6g, of which saturates 4.3g; Cholesterol 381mg; Calcium 115mg; Fibre 0.2g; Sodium 145mg.

VARIATION
Vary the herbs according to what you have available.

PARSLEY AND GARLIC MUSHROOMS ON TOAST

Everybody loves garlic mushrooms. This deluxe version uses big, juicy flat mushrooms, heaped on griddled chewy country bread and topped off with plenty of freshly chopped parsley.

Serves 4

*4 large slices of country
    (preferably sourdough) bread
75g/3oz/6 tbsp butter, plus
    extra melted butter
3 shallots, finely chopped
2 garlic cloves, finely chopped
675g/1½lb field (portobello) or
    chestnut mushrooms, thickly
    sliced
75ml/5 tbsp dry white wine,
    optional
45ml/3 tbsp fresh parsley,
    chopped
salt and ground black pepper*

Energy 297kcal/1240kJ; Protein 8.2g;
Carbohydrate 25.9g, of which sugars 2.9g;
Fat 17.3g, of which saturates 10.2g;
Cholesterol 40mg; Calcium 107mg; Fibre
3.3g; Sodium 420mg.

Toast the bread on both sides on a hot ridged griddle. This will give the bread a striped charred effect as if done on a barbecue. If you don't have a griddle, toast the bread under a hot grill (broiler) on both sides until quite dark. Brush the toasted bread with the extra melted butter and keep warm.

Melt the butter in a frying pan, add the shallots and garlic, and cook for 5 minutes. Add the mushrooms and toss well. Fry over a high heat for 1 minute. Pour over the wine (if using) and season well. Keep the heat high and cook until the wine evaporates. Lightly stir in the parsley. Pile the mushrooms on to the bread and serve immediately.

GARLIC AND HERB BREAD

Excellent with soups or vegetable first courses, garlic bread is also irresistible just on its own. The better the bread, the better the final, garlicky version will be.

Serves 3–4

1 baguette or bloomer loaf

For the garlic and herb butter

115g/4oz/½ cup unsalted butter, softened

5–6 large garlic cloves, finely chopped or crushed

30–45ml/2–3 tbsp fresh parsley, chopped

15ml/1 tbsp snipped fresh chives

salt and ground black pepper

Preheat the oven to 200°C/400°F/Gas 6. Make the garlic and herb butter by beating the butter with the garlic, parsley, chives and seasoning.

Cut the bread into 1cm/½in thick diagonal slices, but leave them attached at the base so that the loaf stays intact.

Spread the butter between the slices, being careful not to detach them, and spread any remaining butter over the top of the loaf.

Wrap the loaf in foil and bake for 20–25 minutes, until the garlic and herb butter is melted and the crust is crisp. Cut into slices to serve.

Energy 920kcal/3877kJ; Protein 22.1g;
Carbohydrate 135.1g, of which sugars 7.2g;
Fat 36.2g, of which saturates 20.8g;
Cholesterol 82mg; Calcium 317mg; Fibre
6.3g; Sodium 1714mg.

LEEK SALAD WITH ANCHOVIES, EGGS AND PARSLEY

Chopped hard-boiled eggs and cooked leeks are a classic combination in French-style salads.
This salad is best served with plenty of fresh crusty bread.

Serves 4

675g/1½lb thin or baby leeks,
 trimmed
2 large or 3 medium eggs
50g/2oz good-quality anchovy
 fillets in olive oil, drained
15g/½oz flat-leaf parsley,
 chopped
a few black olives, pitted
salt and ground black pepper

For the dressing

5ml/1 tsp Dijon mustard
15ml/1 tbsp tarragon vinegar
75ml/5 tbsp olive oil
30ml/2 tbsp double (heavy)
 cream
1 small shallot, very finely
 chopped
pinch of caster (superfine) sugar
 (optional)

Energy 265kcal/1099kJ; Protein 9.4g;
Carbohydrate 6.3g, of which sugars 4.8g;
Fat 22.7g, of which saturates 5.6g;
Cholesterol 113mg; Calcium 107mg; Fibre
4.1g; Sodium 533mg.

Cook the leeks in boiling salted water for 3–4 minutes. Drain, plunge into cold water, then drain again. Squeeze out the excess water, and pat dry.

Place the eggs in a saucepan of cold water, bring to the boil and cook for 6–7 minutes. Drain, plunge into cold water for 10 minutes, then shell and chop the eggs.

To make the dressing, whisk the mustard with the vinegar. Gradually whisk in the oil, followed by the cream. Stir in the shallot, then season to taste with salt, pepper and a pinch of caster sugar, if liked.

Leave the leeks whole or thickly slice them, then place in a serving dish. Pour most of the dressing over them and stir to mix. Leave in a cool place for at least 1 hour, or until ready to serve.

Arrange the anchovies on the leeks, then scatter the eggs and parsley over the top. Drizzle with the remaining dressing, season with black pepper and dot with a few olives. Serve immediately.

FISH AND SEAFOOD

ITS MILD, PLEASANT FLAVOUR MAKES PARSLEY AN

ESSENTIAL INGREDIENT WHEN COOKING WITH

FISH. SAUCES, STEAMED FILLETS AND TASTY

COOKED SHELLFISH WOULD ALL BE INCOMPLETE

WITHOUT THIS FRESH GREEN HERB

SALTED AND GRILLED SARDINES

Whole grilled sardines are classic Mediterranean food, evoking memories of lazy lunches in the sun. Here they are served with a parsley and tarragon salsa pounded with sea salt.

Serves 4–8

8 sardines, total weight about 800g/1¾lb, scaled and gutted
50g/2oz/¼ cup salt
focaccia, to serve
oil, for brushing

For the herb salsa

5ml/1 tsp sea salt flakes
60ml/4 tbsp chopped fresh tarragon leaves
40g/1½oz/generous 1 cup flat-leaf parsley, chopped
1 small red onion, very finely chopped
105ml/7 tbsp extra virgin olive oil
60ml/4 tbsp lemon juice

Energy 327kcal/1362kJ; Protein 35g;
Carbohydrate 0.3g, of which sugars 0.3g;
Fat 20.5g, of which saturates 8g;
Cholesterol 16mg; Calcium 192mg; Fibre
0.5g; Sodium 240mg.

Rub the sardines inside and out with salt. Cover and put in a cool place for 30–45 minutes. Make the salsa by adding the salt to a mortar and pounding in all the ingredients one at a time with a pestle.

Meanwhile, prepare the barbecue. Rinse the salt off the sardines. Pat them dry with kitchen paper, then leave to air-dry for 15 minutes. Once the flames have died down, position a lightly oiled grill rack over the coals to heat.

When the coals are cool, or with a thick coating of ash, brush the fish with a little oil and put them in a small, hinged, wire barbecue fish basket. If you don't have a wire basket, grill directly on the rack, but oil it well first. Grill for about 3 minutes on one side and about 2½ minutes on the other. Serve with the herb salsa and focaccia.

MUSSELS WITH A PARSLEY CRUST

In this delectable recipe succulent mussels are grilled with a fragrant topping of Parmesan cheese,
garlic and parsley, which helps to prevent the mussels from becoming overcooked.

Serves 4

450g/1lb fresh mussels
90ml/6 tbsp water
15ml/1 tbsp melted butter
15ml/1 tbsp olive oil
45ml/3 tbsp freshly grated
*   Parmesan cheese*
30ml/2 tbsp fresh parsley,
*   chopped*
2 garlic cloves, finely chopped
2.5ml/½ tsp coarsely ground
*   black pepper*
crusty bread, to serve

Scrub the mussels thoroughly, scraping off any barnacles with a round-bladed knife and pulling out the gritty beards. Sharply tap any open mussels and discard any that fail to close or whose shells are broken.

Place the mussels in a large pan and add the water. Cover the pan with a lid and steam for about 5 minutes, or until the mussel shells have opened.

Drain the mussels well and discard any that remain closed. Carefully snap off the top shell from each mussel, leaving the actual flesh still attached to the bottom shell.

Balance the shells in a flameproof dish, packing them closely together to make sure that they stay level.

Preheat the grill (broiler) to high. Put the melted butter, olive oil, grated Parmesan cheese, parsley, garlic and black pepper in a small bowl and mix well to combine.

Spoon a small amount of the cheese and garlic mixture on top of each mussel and gently press down with the back of the spoon.

Grill (broil) the mussels for about 2 minutes, or until they are sizzling and golden. Serve the mussels in their shells, with plenty of bread to mop up the delicious juices.

Energy 110kcal/456kJ; Protein 5.4g; Carbohydrate 0.3g, of which sugars 0.3g; Fat 9.7g, of which saturates 4.7g; Cholesterol 21mg; Calcium 165mg; Fibre 0.6g; Sodium 156mg.

COOK'S TIP

Give each guest one of the discarded top shells of the mussels. They can be used as a little spoon to free the body from the shell of the next. Scoop up the mussel in the empty shell and tip the shellfish and topping into your mouth.

FISHCAKES WITH CURRANTS, PINE NUTS AND HERBS

Whether served as a starter or as a main course with a salad, these fresh, tasty fishcakes are delicious flavoured with cinnamon and the herbs parsley, mint and dill.

Serves 4

450g/1lb skinless fresh white fish fillets

2 slices of day-old bread, briefly sprinkled with water, then squeezed dry

1 red onion, finely chopped

30ml/2 tbsp currants, soaked in warm water for 5–10 minutes and drained

30ml/2 tbsp pine nuts

1 small bunch each of fresh flat-leaf parsley, mint and dill, finely chopped

1 egg

5–10ml/1–2 tsp tomato purée (paste) or ketchup

15ml/1 tbsp ground cinnamon

45–60ml/3–4 tbsp plain (all-purpose) flour

45–60ml/3–4 tbsp sunflower oil

salt and ground black pepper

1 small bunch fresh flat-leaf parsley and 1–2 lemons, cut into wedges, to serve

In a bowl, break up the fish with a fork. Add the bread, onion, currants and pine nuts, toss in the herbs and mix well.

In another small bowl, beat the egg with the tomato purée and 10ml/2 tsp of the cinnamon. Pour the mixture over the fish and season with salt and pepper, then mix with your hands and mould into small balls.

Mix the flour on a plate with the remaining 5 ml/1 tsp cinnamon. Press each ball into a flat cake and coat in the flour.

Heat the oil in a wide, shallow pan and fry the fishcakes in batches for 8–10 minutes, until golden brown. Lift out and drain on kitchen paper. Serve hot on a bed of parsley, with lemon wedges for squeezing.

Energy 317kcal/1324kJ; Protein 26.1g; Carbohydrate 17.8g, of which sugars 2.5g; Fat 16.2g, of which saturates 1.9g; Cholesterol 99mg; Calcium 79mg; Fibre 1.6g; Sodium 169mg.

SEA BASS WITH PARSLEY AND LIME BUTTER

The delicate but firm, sweet flesh of sea bass goes beautifully with citrus flavours and fresh parsley.
Serve with roast fennel and sautéed diced potatoes.

Serves 6

50g/2oz/¼ cup butter
6 sea bass fillets, about
*   150g/5oz each*
grated rind and juice of 1 large
*   lime*
30ml/2 tbsp fresh parsley,
*   chopped*
salt and ground black pepper

Energy 214kcal/894kJ; Protein 29.2g;
Carbohydrate 0.2g, of which sugars 0.2g;
Fat 10.7g, of which saturates 4.9g;
Cholesterol 138mg; Calcium 207mg; Fibre
0.3g; Sodium 156mg.

Heat half the butter in a large frying pan and add three of the sea bass fillets, skin side down. Cook for 3–4 minutes, or until the skin is crisp and golden. Flip the fish over and cook for a further 2–3 minutes, or until cooked through.

Remove the fillets from the pan with a metal spatula. Place each on a serving plate and keep them warm. Cook the remaining fish in the same way and transfer to serving plates.

Add the lime rind and juice to the pan with the parsley, and season with salt and black pepper. Allow to bubble for 1–2 minutes, then pour a little over each fish portion and serve immediately.

HALIBUT FILLET WITH PARSLEY SAUCE

This beautifully simple dish is often served with steamed cauliflower and buttered new potatoes, but steamed shredded green cabbage or braised leeks would also work well.

Serves 4
900g/2lb halibut fillet
2 eggs, beaten
10ml/2 tsp water
75g/3oz/1½ cup fine
   breadcrumbs
10ml/2 tsp salt
2.5ml/½ tsp white pepper
50g/2oz/4 tbsp butter
4 lemon wedges, to garnish

For the parsley sauce
50g/2oz/4 tbsp butter
60ml/4 tbsp plain (all-purpose)
   flour
350ml/12fl oz/1½ cups milk
45ml/3tbsp fresh parsley, finely
   chopped
salt

Cut the halibut into four pieces. Whisk the eggs and water together in a shallow dish. Place the breadcrumbs in a second shallow dish. Dip the fish into the egg mixture, then into the breadcrumbs, to coat both sides evenly. Sprinkle with salt and pepper.

To make the parsley sauce, melt the butter in a pan over a medium heat, and whisk in the flour. Reduce the heat and cook the roux for 3–5 minutes. Slowly add the milk into the roux; cook, whisking constantly until the sauce comes to the boil and is smooth and thick. Season, add the parsley and simmer for 2 minutes. Cover and keep warm.

Melt the butter in a large pan over a medium-high heat. Place the halibut fillets in the pan, and cook for about 4 minutes on each side, turning once, until the coating is golden brown and the fish flakes easily with a fork. Serve the halibut fillets with the sauce spooned over.

Energy 594kcal/2493kJ; Protein 58.2g;
Carbohydrate 30.4g, of which sugars 5g;
Fat 27.6g, of which saturates 14.1g;
Cholesterol 227mg; Calcium 234mg; Fibre
0.9g; Sodium 487mg.

PAN-FRIED DOVER SOLE WITH PARSLEY

For many, Dover sole is one of the finest of the flat fish, and is best cooked very simply under a grill or broiler, or lightly fried, as here . The fresh parsley adds flavour and colour to the dish.

Serves 4

30–45ml/2–3 tbsp plain (all-purpose) flour seasoned with salt and pepper

4 small Dover sole, dark skin and fins removed

45ml/3 tbsp olive oil

25g/1oz/2 tbsp butter

juice of 1 lemon

15ml/1 tbsp fresh parsley, chopped

watercress sprigs and slice of lemon, to garnish

Spread the seasoned flour on a plate, and coat each fish, shaking off any excess. Heat a large non-stick frying pan and add the oil.

Add one or two fish to the pan and cook over a medium heat for 3–5 minutes on each side until golden brown and cooked through. Lift them out and keep them warm while you cook the remaining fish.

Add the butter to the hot pan and heat until the butter has melted. Stir in the lemon juice and chopped parsley. Drizzle the pan juices over the fish and serve immediately on warmed plates, garnished with watercress sprigs and a slice of lemon.

COOK'S TIP
Leaving the white skin on one side of the fish helps to keep its shape during cooking; it is also full of flavour and good to eat, particularly the crisp edges.

Energy 177kcal/739kJ; Protein 18.6g; Carbohydrate 3g, of which sugars 0.2g; Fat 10.2g, of which saturates 1.2g; Cholesterol 50mg; Calcium 42mg; Fibre 0.3g; Sodium 101mg

MEAT AND POULTRY

PARSLEY ENLIVENS STUFFINGS AND COATINGS
AND IS A WONDERFUL ADDITION TO ALL MEATS
AND POULTRY. FROM ROAST MEATS AND FRIED
PATTIES TO HEARTY CASSEROLES AND WINTER
PIES, PARSLEY HAS AN IMPORTANT ROLE TO PLAY

LAMB CASSEROLE WITH PARSLEY AND BROAD BEANS

This recipe has a Spanish influence and makes a substantial meal, served with potatoes. It's based on stewing lamb with a large amount of garlic and sherry – the addition of parsley gives colour.

Serves 6

45ml/3 tbsp olive oil
1.5kg/3–3½lb lamb fillet, cut into 5cm/2in cubes
1 large onion, chopped
6 large garlic cloves, unpeeled
1 bay leaf
5ml/1 tsp paprika
120ml/4fl oz/½ cup dry sherry
115g/4oz shelled fresh or frozen broad (fava) beans
30ml/2 tbsp fresh parsley, chopped
salt and ground black pepper

Energy 541kcal/2258kJ; Protein 50.8g;
Carbohydrate 3.5g, of which sugars 1.2g;
Fat 33.7g, of which saturates 13.8g;
Cholesterol 190mg; Calcium 45mg; Fibre
1.6g; Sodium 221mg.

Heat 30ml/2 tbsp of the oil in a large flameproof casserole. Add half the meat and brown well on all sides. Transfer to a plate. Brown the rest of the meat in the same way and remove from the casserole.

Heat the remaining oil in the pan, add the onion and cook for about 5 minutes until soft. Return the meat to the casserole.

Add the garlic cloves, bay leaf, paprika and sherry. Season with salt and pepper. Bring to the boil, then cover and simmer very gently for 1½–2 hours, until the meat is tender.

Add the broad beans about 10 minutes before the end of the cooking time. Stir in the parsley just before serving.

BULGUR AND LAMB PATTIES

Both the Lebanese and the Syrians claim these meatballs as their own. There are numerous variations – this one uses fragrant lamb and bulgur wheat, flavoured with fresh flat-leaf parsley.

Serves 6

*225g/8oz/1¼ cups bulgur
    wheat, rinsed and drained
450g/1lb lean lamb, cut into
    small chunks
2 onions, grated
5–10ml/1–2 tsp ground allspice
5–10ml/1–2 tsp paprika
10ml/2 tsp ground cumin
5–10ml/1–2 tsp salt
1 bunch parsley, finely chopped,
    plus extra to garnish
sunflower oil, for frying
ground black pepper
1–2 lemons, cut into wedges, to
    serve*

Energy 407kcal/1694kJ; Protein 20.1g;
Carbohydrate 35.9g, of which sugars 3.9g;
Fat 20.9g, of which saturates 5.3g;
Cholesterol 57mg; Calcium 65mg; Fibre
1.4g; Sodium 400mg

Tip the bulgur into a bowl and pour in just enough boiling water to cover it. Cover the bowl with a clean dish towel and leave the bulgur for 20 minutes to swell.

Put the lamb into a food processor and grind to a paste. Turn it into a bowl and add the onion, spices and parsley, with salt and a generous amount of pepper.

Squeeze any excess water from the bulgur and grind it to a paste in the food processor. Add it to the bowl and use your hands to mix everything together and knead well. Process the mixture again and return it to the bowl for further kneading.

With wet hands, divide the mixture into small balls and flatten each one in the palm of your hand. Heat enough oil for frying in a shallow pan and cook the patties in batches, about 3 minutes on each side, until nicely browned. Drain on kitchen paper and serve hot with lemon wedges to squeeze over them, garnished with parsley.

BACON WITH CABBAGE AND PARSLEY SAUCE

*This recipe is a modern rendition of a great old Irish favourite and brings together a number of classic
ingredients. Traditional accompaniments include boiled or mashed swede.*

Serves 6

*1.3kg/3lb loin of bacon
1 carrot, chopped
2 celery sticks, chopped
2 leeks, chopped
5ml/1 tsp peppercorns
15ml/1 tbsp yellow mustard
15ml/1 tbsp oven-dried
   breadcrumbs
7.5ml/1½ tsp light muscovado
   (brown) sugar
25g/1oz/2 tbsp butter
900g/2lb green cabbage, sliced*

For the parsley sauce

*50g/2oz/¼ cup butter
25g/1oz/¼ cup plain
   (all-purpose) flour
150ml/¼ pint/⅔ cup single
   (light) cream
bunch of parsley, leaves
   chopped
salt and ground black pepper*

Place the bacon joint in a large pan. Add the vegetables to the pan,
with the peppercorns. Cover with cold water and bring to the boil.
Simmer gently for about 20 minutes per 450g/1lb. Preheat the oven
to 200°C/400°F/Gas 6.

Remove the joint from the pan, reserving 150ml/¼ pint/⅔ cup of
the cooking liquid. Remove the rind, and score the fat. Place the joint
in a roasting pan. Mix the mustard, breadcrumbs, sugar and 15g/½oz/1
tbsp butter; spread this mixture over the joint. Place in the oven for
15–20 minutes.

To make the parsley sauce, melt the butter in a small pan, then add
the flour and cook for 1–2 minutes, stirring constantly. Whisk in the
cooking liquid and cream. Bring to the boil. Reduce the heat and simmer
for 3–4 minutes, then stir in the chopped fresh parsley. Season to taste
with salt and pepper. The sauce should have the consistency of thin
cream. Keep warm.

In another pan cook the cabbage with a little of the cooking liquid
from the bacon. Drain well, season to taste and toss in the remaining
butter.

To serve, slice the bacon and serve on a bed of cabbage, with the
parsley sauce.

Energy 689kcal/2857kJ; Protein 40.4g; Carbohydrate 16.3g, of which sugars 10.6g; Fat 51.5g,
of which saturates 23.1g; Cholesterol 155mg; Calcium 139mg; Fibre 5g; Sodium 3461mg.

BEEF AND SWEET POTATO SALAD WITH HERB DRESSING

This salad makes a good main dish for a summer buffet, especially if the beef has been cut into fork-size strips. It is absolutely delicious with a simple potato salad and some peppery leaves.

Serves 6–8
800g/1¾lb fillet of beef
5ml/1 tsp black peppercorns,
    crushed
10ml/2 tsp chopped fresh thyme
60ml/4 tbsp olive oil
450g/1lb orange-fleshed sweet
    potato, peeled
salt and ground black pepper

For the herb dressing
1 garlic clove, chopped
15g/½oz fresh parsley, chopped
30ml/2 tbsp chopped fresh
    coriander (cilantro)
15ml/1 tbsp small salted
    capers, rinsed
½–1 fresh green chilli, seeded
    and chopped
10ml/2 tsp Dijon mustard
10–15ml/2–3 tsp white wine
    vinegar
75ml/5 tbsp extra virgin olive oil
2 shallots, finely chopped

Roll the beef fillet in the crushed peppercorns and thyme, then set aside to marinate for a few hours. Preheat the oven to 200°C/400°F/Gas 6.

Heat half the olive oil in a heavy-based frying pan. Add the beef and brown it all over, turning frequently, to seal it. Place on a baking tray and cook in the oven for 10–15 minutes.

Remove the beef from the oven, and cover with foil, then leave to rest for 10–15 minutes.

Meanwhile, preheat the grill (broiler). Cut the sweet potatoes into 1cm/½in slices. Brush with the remaining olive oil, season to taste with salt and pepper, and grill (broil) for about 5–6 minutes on each side, until tender and browned. Cut the sweet potato slices into strips and place them in a large bowl.

Cut the beef into slices or strips and toss with the sweet potato, then set the bowl aside.

For the dressing, process the garlic, parsley, fresh coriander, capers, chilli, mustard and 10ml/2 tsp of the vinegar in a food processor or blender until chopped. With the motor still running, gradually pour in the oil to make a smooth dressing. Season the dressing with salt and pepper and add more vinegar, to taste. Stir in the shallots.

Toss the dressing into the sweet potatoes and beef and leave to stand for up to 2 hours before serving

Energy 300kcal/1253kJ; Protein 26g; Carbohydrate 12g, of which sugars 3.2g; Fat 18.6g, of which saturates 4.6g; Cholesterol 61mg; Calcium 18mg; Fibre 1.4g; Sodium 67mg

CHICKEN WITH PARSLEY STUFFING

These little chicken drumsticks have a delectable herby flavour, in which parsley predominates.
The slices of bacon keep the chicken wonderfully moist during cooking.

Serves 4

60ml/4 tbsp ricotta cheese
1 garlic clove, crushed
30ml/2 tbsp fresh parsley,
    chopped
15ml/1 tbsp mixed chopped
    fresh chives and tarragon
5ml/1 tsp chopped fresh mint
30ml/2 tbsp fresh brown
    breadcrumbs
8 chicken drumsticks
8 smoked streaky bacon slices
5ml/1 tsp wholegrain mustard
15ml/1 tbsp sunflower oil
salt and ground black pepper
chopped fresh parsley and
    chives, to garnish

Mix together the ricotta, garlic, herbs, breadcrumbs and seasoning. Carefully loosen the skin of each drumstick and spoon a little of the herb stuffing under the skin. Smooth the skin firmly over the stuffing.

Wrap a slice of bacon around the wide end of each drumstick, to hold the skin in place over the stuffing.

Mix together the mustard and oil and brush over the chicken. Cook over a medium-hot barbecue for about 25 minutes, turning occasionally, until the chicken is cooked through and the meat juices run clear. Serve garnished with chopped parsley and chives.

Energy 268kcal/1114kJ; Protein 24g; Carbohydrate 6g, of which sugars 4g; Fat 20g, of which saturates 9g; Cholesterol 122mg; Calcium 87mg; Fibre 0.9g; Sodium 205mg

COOK'S TIP
If you can't use the barbecue, cook indoors in the oven at 180°C/350°F/Gas 4 for 25–30 minutes, turning occasionally.

CHICKEN, LEEK AND PARSLEY PIE

This tasty pie is good served hot, warm or cold and is ideal for picnics. If you prefer, you could make four individual pies in small tart tins or in a four-hole muffin tin.

Serves 4
400g/14oz shortcrust pastry,
    thawed if frozen
15g/½oz/1 tbsp butter
1 leek, thinly sliced
2 eggs
225g/8oz skinless chicken
    breast fillets, finely chopped
1 small handful of fresh parsley,
    chopped
salt and ground black pepper
beaten egg, to glaze

VARIATION
The pies are just as nice made with puff pastry instead of shortcrust.

Energy 588kcal/2459kJ; Protein 23.4g;
Carbohydrate 48.4g, of which sugars 2.1g;
Fat 34.9g, of which saturates 11.7g;
Cholesterol 157mg; Calcium 133mg; Fibre
3.4g; Sodium 496mg

Preheat the oven to 200°C/400°F/Gas 6. Roll out the pastry on a lightly floured surface to a thickness of about 3mm/⅛in. Cut out a circle large enough to line a 20cm/8in tart tin (pan) and line the pan. Cut the remaining pastry into a slightly smaller circle ready to make a lid for the pie.

Melt the butter in a small pan, add the leek and cook gently for about 5 minutes, stirring occasionally, until soft but not brown.

Beat the eggs in a bowl and stir in the chicken, parsley and seasoning. Add the leek and its juices from the pan, stirring until well mixed.

Spoon the mixture into the pastry case, filling it generously. Brush the edges of the pastry with beaten egg and place the lid on top, pressing the edges together to seal it. Brush the top of the pie with beaten egg and make a small slit in the centre to allow steam to escape.

Put into the hot oven and cook for about 30 minutes, until golden brown and cooked through.

VEGETARIAN AND SIDE DISHES

PARSLEY IS PERFECT FOR SUBTLE

VEGETABLE DISHES. WHETHER USED IN SAUCES

OR STARRING IN SALADS, THIS VERSATILE HERB

ADDS VIBRANT COLOUR WITH ITS UNASSUMING

BUT MUCH-LOVED FLAVOUR

TABBOULEH

This is a wonderfully refreshing, tangy salad of soaked bulgur wheat and masses of fresh mint, parsley and spring onions. Feel free to increase the amount of herbs for a greener salad.

Serves 4–6

250g/9oz/1½ cups bulgur wheat
1 large bunch spring onions (scallions), thinly sliced
1 cucumber, finely chopped or diced
3 tomatoes, chopped
1.5–2.5ml/¼–½ tsp ground cumin
1 bunch fresh parsley, chopped
1 bunch fresh mint, chopped
juice of 2 lemons, or to taste
60ml/4 tbsp extra virgin olive oil
salt
olives, lemon wedges, tomato wedges, cucumber slices and mint sprigs, to garnish
cos or romaine lettuce and natural (plain) yogurt, to serve

Pick over the bulgur to remove any dirt. Place it in a bowl, cover with cold water and leave to soak for about 30 minutes. Tip the bulgur wheat into a sieve and drain well, shaking to remove any excess water, then return it to the bowl.

Add the spring onions to the bulgur, then mix and squeeze together with your hands to combine.

Add the cucumber, tomatoes, cumin, parsley, mint, lemon juice, oil and salt to taste to the bulgur and toss to combine.

Heap the tabbouleh on to a bed of lettuce and garnish with olives, lemon wedges, tomato, cucumber and mint sprigs. Serve with a bowl of natural yogurt.

Energy 232kcal/965kJ; Protein 5.2g; Carbohydrate 34.6g, of which sugars 2.7g; Fat 8.4g, of which saturates 1.1g; Cholesterol 0mg; Calcium 51mg; Fibre 1.4g; Sodium 12mg.

COUSCOUS SALAD

This classic Moroccan salad is flavoured with almonds, parsley and fresh coriander (cilantro). It has a delicate taste and is excellent with grilled chicken or kebabs.

Serves 4

275g/10oz/1²⁄₃ cups couscous
525ml/18fl oz/2¼ cups boiling
    vegetable stock
16–20 black olives
2 small courgettes (zucchini)
25g/1oz/¼ cup flaked almonds,
    toasted
60ml/4 tbsp olive oil
15ml/1 tbsp lemon juice
30ml/2 tbsp fresh parsley,
    chopped
15ml/1 tbsp fresh coriander
    (cilantro), chopped
good pinch of ground cumin
good pinch of cayenne pepper
salt

Energy 123kcal/509kJ; Protein 1g;
Carbohydrate 4g, of which sugars 4g; Fat
12g, of which saturates 2g; Cholesterol
0mg; Calcium 44mg; Fibre 1g; Sodium
176mg.

Place the couscous in a bowl and pour over the boiling stock. Stir with a fork and then set aside for 10 minutes for the stock to be absorbed. Fluff up with a fork.

Halve the olives, discarding the stones. Top and tail the courgettes and cut into small julienne strips.

Carefully mix the courgettes, olives and almonds into the couscous.

Blend together the olive oil, lemon juice, herbs, spices and a pinch of salt and stir into the salad.

PARSLEY SALAD WITH BULGUR

The main ingredient of this Lebanese salad is parsley, flavoured with a hint of mint and tossed with a little fine bulgur wheat so that the grains resemble tiny gems in a sea of green.

Serves 4–6

65g/2½oz/½ cup fine bulgur
    wheat
juice of 2 lemons
1 large bunch flat-leaf parsley
a handful of fresh mint leaves
2–3 tomatoes, skinned, seeded
    and finely diced
4 spring onions (scallions),
    trimmed and finely sliced
60ml/4 tbsp olive oil
salt and ground black pepper
1 cos or romaine lettuce,
    trimmed and split into leaves,
    to serve

Energy 232kcal/965kJ; Protein 5.2g;
Carbohydrate 34.6g, of which sugars 2.7g;
Fat 8.4g, of which saturates 1.1g;
Cholesterol 0mg; Calcium 51mg; Fibre
1.4g; Sodium 12mg

Rinse the bulgur in cold water and drain well. Place it in a bowl and pour over the lemon juice. Leave to soften for 10 minutes while you prepare the salad.

With the parsley tightly bunched, slice the leaves as finely as you can with a sharp knife. Transfer the parsley into a bowl. Slice the mint leaves and add them to the bowl with the tomatoes, spring onions and the soaked bulgur. Pour in the oil, season with salt and pepper and toss the salad gently.

Serve immediately, so that the herbs do not get the chance to soften. Arrange the lettuce leaves around the salad and use them to scoop up the salad.

HERBY VEGETABLE PATTIES

Ideal for lunch, supper, a savoury snack or appetizer, these tasty Turkish patties are incredibly versatile. You can even make miniature ones and serve them as a nibble with drinks.

Serves 4–6

3 firm courgettes (zucchini)
30–45ml/2–3 tbsp olive oil
1 large onion, cut in half lengthways, in half again crossways, and sliced along the grain
4 garlic cloves, chopped
45ml/3 tbsp plain (all-purpose) flour
3 eggs, beaten
225g/8oz feta cheese, crumbled
1 bunch each of fresh flat leaf parsley, mint and dill, chopped
5ml/1 tsp Turkish red pepper, or 1 fresh red chilli, seeded and chopped
sunflower oil, for shallow frying
salt and ground black pepper
mint leaves, to garnish

Wash the courgettes and trim off the ends. Hold them at an angle and grate them, then put them in a colander or sieve (strainer) and sprinkle with a little salt. Leave them to sweat for 5 minutes.

Squeeze the grated courgettes in your hand to extract the juices. Heat the olive oil in a heavy frying pan, stir in the courgettes, onion and garlic and fry until they begin to take on colour. Remove from the heat and leave to cool.

Tip the flour into a bowl and gradually beat in the eggs to form a smooth batter. Beat in the cooled courgette mixture. Add the feta, herbs and red pepper or chilli, and season with a little pepper. Add salt if you like, but usually the feta is quite salty. Mix well.

Heat enough sunflower oil for shallow frying in a heavy, non-stick pan. Drop four spoonfuls of the mixture into the hot oil, leaving space between each one, then fry over a medium heat for 6–8 minutes, or until firm to the touch and golden brown on both sides. Remove from the pan with a slotted spoon and drain on kitchen paper while you fry the remainder.

Serve while still warm, garnished with mint leaves.

Energy 327kcal/1354kJ; Protein 12.3g;
Carbohydrate 12.4g, of which sugars 5.4g;
Fat 25.7g, of which saturates 7.9g;
Cholesterol 121mg; Calcium 214mg; Fibre
2.3g; Sodium 581mg.

BAKED FENNEL WITH A HERBY CRUMB CRUST

Garlic and parsley blend perfectly with the delicate, aniseed flavour of fennel in this tasty gratin.
It goes well with pasta dishes and risottos.

Serves 4

3 fennel bulbs, cut lengthways
    into quarters
30ml/2 tbsp olive oil
1 garlic clove, chopped
50g/2oz/1 cup day-old
    wholemeal (whole-wheat)
    breadcrumbs
30ml/2 tbsp fresh flat-leaf
    parsley, chopped
salt and ground black pepper
fennel leaves, to garnish

VARIATION

To make a cheese-topped version of this dish, simply add 60ml/4 tbsp finely grated strong-flavoured cheese, such as mature Cheddar, Red Leicester, or Parmesan, to the breadcrumb mixture. Sprinkle the mixture over the fennel as described.

Cook the fennel in a pan of boiling salted water for 10 minutes, or until just tender.

Drain the fennel quarters and place them in a baking dish or roasting tin (pan), then brush them all over with half of the olive oil. .

Preheat the oven to 190°C/375°F/Gas 5.

In a small bowl, mix together the garlic, breadcrumbs and parsley with the rest of the oil. Sprinkle the mixture evenly over the fennel, then season well with salt and pepper.

Bake for 30 minutes, or until the fennel is tender and the breadcrumbs are crisp and golden. Serve hot, garnished with a few fennel leaves.

Energy 113kcal/471kJ; Protein 3g; Carbohydrate 8g, of which sugars 3g; Fat 8g, of which saturates 1g; Cholesterol 0mg; Calcium 49mg; Fibre 1g; Sodium 77mg.

PARSLEY AND RICOTTA BREAD

Ricotta cheese and parsley make a moist, well-flavoured loaf that is excellent for sandwiches. Shape the dough into rolls, loaves, a cottage loaf, or even a plait.

Makes 1 loaf or 16 rolls

*15g/½oz fresh yeast or 10ml/
    2 tsp active dried yeast*
*5ml/1 tsp caster (superfine)
    sugar*
*270ml/9fl oz/generous 1 cup
    lukewarm water*
*450g/1lb unbleached strong
    white flour, plus a little extra*
7.5ml/1½ tsp salt
1 large egg, beaten
115g/4oz/½ cup ricotta cheese
*1 bunch spring onions
    (scallions), thinly sliced*
30ml/2 tbsp extra virgin olive oil
*45ml/3 tbsp fresh parsley,
    chopped*
15ml/1 tbsp milk
*10ml/2 tsp poppy seeds
    (optional)*
coarse sea salt

Energy 1582kcal/6693kJ; Protein 47.5g;
Carbohydrate 293.7g, of which sugars
11.5g; Fat 32.3g, of which saturates 10.8g;
Cholesterol 41mg; Calcium 824mg; Fibre
14.3g; Sodium 3422mg

Cream the fresh yeast with the sugar and gradually stir in 120ml/ 4fl oz/½ cup of the water. If using dried yeast, stir the sugar into the water, then sprinkle it over the surface. Leave in a warm place for about 10 minutes.

Sift the flour and salt into a warmed bowl. Make a well in the centre and pour in the yeast liquid and the remaining water. Save a little beaten egg, then put the rest in the bowl. Add the ricotta and mix to form a dough, adding a little more flour if the mixture is very sticky.

Knead the dough on a floured work surface until smooth and elastic. Set aside in a greased bowl, inside a polythene bag, in a warm place for 1–2 hours, until doubled in size.

Meanwhile, cook the spring onions in the oil for 3–4 minutes, until soft but not browned. Set aside to cool.

Punch down the risen dough and knead in the onions, with their oil from cooking, and the parsley. Shape the dough into rolls, a large or small loaf, cottage loaf, or a plait.

Grease a baking sheet or loaf tin and place the rolls or bread on it. Cover with oiled clear film (plastic wrap) and leave in a warm place to rise for about 1 hour. Preheat the oven to 200°C/400°F/Gas 6.

Beat the milk into the reserved beaten egg and use to glaze the rolls or loaf. Sprinkle with poppy seeds, if using, and a little coarse sea salt, then bake rolls for about 15 minutes or a loaf for 30–40 minutes or until golden and well risen. When tapped firmly on the base, the bread should feel and sound firm. Cool on a wire rack.

PARMA HAM, PARMESAN AND PARSLEY BREAD

Chopped Parma ham is combined with Parmesan cheese and chopped fresh parsley for a moist, nourishing bread that is almost a meal in itself.

Serves 8

225 g/8 oz/2 cups self-raising wholemeal (whole-wheat) flour
225 g/8 oz/2 cups self-raising (self-rising) white flour
5 ml/1 tsp baking powder
5 ml/1 tsp salt
5 ml/1 tsp freshly ground black pepper
75 g/3 oz Parma ham, chopped
25 g/1 oz/2 tbsp freshly grated Parmesan cheese
30 ml/2 tbsp fresh parsley, chopped
45 ml/3 tbsp Meaux mustard
350 ml/12 fl oz/1½ cups buttermilk
skimmed milk, to glaze

Preheat the oven to 200°C/400°F/Gas 6. Flour a baking sheet. Place the wholemeal flour in a bowl and sift in the white flour, baking powder and salt. Add the pepper and the ham. Set aside about 15 ml/1 tbsp of the grated Parmesan and stir the rest into the flour mixture. Stir in the parsley. Make a well in the centre.

Mix the mustard and buttermilk in a jug, pour into the flour mixture and quickly mix to a soft dough.

Turn the dough on to a floured surface and knead briefly. Shape into an oval loaf, brush with milk and sprinkle with the remaining cheese. Place the loaf on the prepared baking sheet.

Bake the loaf for 25–30 minutes, or until golden brown. Transfer to a wire rack to cool.

Energy 229kcal/972kJ; Protein 11.1g; Carbohydrate 42.4g, of which sugars 3.5g; Fat 2.9g, of which saturates 1g; Cholesterol 10mg; Calcium 146mg; Fibre 3.4g; Sodium 334mg.

INDEX